Paws and Prayers

for: *John*

May God bless you and all the four-legged friends
that are special to you.

from: *Margaret*

Photo: James Groundwater

Then God commanded, ... the earth produce ... animal life:
domestic and w ... ... ne.
So God made them ... ... ie saw.

A lifelong friendship

"Blessed is the man who does not fall away on account of me."
Matthew 11:6 (NIV)

It's a hard nut who doesn't go all gooey at the sight of a kitten or puppy.

There is something about a baby animal that inevitably brings out the soft side in us. We feel a warm glow of happiness and suddenly the world doesn't seem such a bad place after all. "Aren't they cute?" someone will say with a smile. "What a pity they have to grow up."

Both our dogs are rescue dogs. Rescue centres are awash with dogs and cats and various other animals who all find themselves there because their owners can't cope. Sometimes it's because their owner has died. Often it's because the animal was bought or given as a puppy or kitten and once the novelty wore off and the animal grew up, the time and commitment – not to mention the cost – of owning a pet proved too much hassle. Puppies and kittens are cute, but we've all seen the car sticker, 'A dog is for life, not just for Christmas'.

Each Christmas, church congregations swell as people attend carol services and Midnight Mass. It's wonderful that folk come to worship the heavenly babe, born in Bethlehem. Sadly, however, the majority of them will leave the infant Christ in the manger once Christmas is over. The baby Jesus will have given them a warm glow; a sense of peace and goodwill, but the feeling is short-lived. Why? Because people won't allow the baby to grow into the man who can do so much for them.

For them, the adult Christ presents too much of challenge. He asks for commitment and demands more of them than they are prepared to give.

That's a shame. The baby might make us go all gooey, but it's the adult – in the case of both Jesus and the dog – who offers protection, life-long friendship and unconditional love.

Lord Jesus, the celebration of your birth touches people the world over! But it was your ministry as an adult that transformed the world forever. May we share the joy of your whole life and help people to accept Jesus the man into their hearts and homes.

Photo: Meryl Vincent-Enright

Photo: Jonathan Merrell

Feeling threatened?

But the fruit of the Spirit is love, joy, peace, patience, kindness, goodness, faithfulness, gentleness and self-control. Against such things there is no law.

Galatians 5:22-23 (NIV)

•

Our new dog, Milli, watches television. Yes, she really does. She's not very selective and can't use the remote control yet, but she knows what she likes. Rather, she knows what she doesn't like. She doesn't like other dogs on the box. The moment she sees one, or hears one bark, she's there, growling at the screen. She doesn't realise the dogs aren't real – just virtual images as we say – she barks anyway.

We used to have a dog who disliked opera singers, particularly tenors. Whether it was Placido Domingo, or Pavarotti or Carreras, it was all the same to him. When he heard them sing he sat in front of the telly, head in air, and howled.

But back to Milli. It's not only dogs. Anything large that moves quickly across the screen disturbs her. She just doesn't understand that the threat isn't real, there's no danger. I know people like Milli. People who feel threatened by anything or anyone new or different. And whatever they don't understand they do the human equivalent of barking at it. Even if there's no real threat.

But if I look honestly at myself, I'll find I sometimes do the same. But it's better to be positive, to welcome the new and the different, and think twice before we bark. Or even learn not to bark at all. That's our next job in training Milli.

By Eddie Askew, taken from *Chasing the Leaves,* published by The Leprosy Mission

Lord, things change so fast these days and sometimes it's difficult to keep up. Help me to accept new challenges, fresh faces and different ways of doing things – they might even be an improvement.

All things bright and beautiful
All creatures great and small,
All things wise and wonderful.
The Lord God made them all.

He gave us eyes to see them,
And lips that we might tell,
How great is God Almighty,
Who has made all things well.

Mrs Cecil Frances Alexander
1818–1895, Irish hymn writer

Old dogs, new tricks

So get rid of your old self, which made you live as you used to – the old self
that was being destroyed by its deceitful desires. Your hearts and minds must
be made completely new, and you must put on the new self, which is created
in God's likeness and reveals itself in the true life that is upright and holy.

Ephesians 4:22-24 (GNB)

●

Our hounds are aged eleven and ten. What they haven't learnt by now, they probably
never will. I'm partly to blame; if I'd taken the time and had the patience when they
were pups, I might be leading them around the arena at Crufts instead of having my
arm yanked out of its socket when we go for walkies.

Blossom, in particular, is determined that I will go to my grave with one arm longer than
the other. She might be small, but she's wilful and cannot – or will not – resist pulling
every inch of the way. I've tried various approaches in an attempt to make her walk to
heel, all to no avail. If you see a woman with a small black-and-white dog walking at
45 degrees, chances are it's Blossom and me.

It really does seem that the old adage is true; you can't teach an old dog new tricks.
Whatever they learn, is learnt when they are young and flexible and their owner/trainer
is patient and persistent.

Fortunately for the human race, it's never too late to learn, even when it comes to a
complete rethink about our attitude to life, love and the universe. Once we've been
introduced to Jesus, and accepted his guidance, even our worst and most deep-rooted
habits can be changed and our negative qualities turned into positives.

God's grace knows no bounds. Even hardened criminals have had their lives turned
around by his love and mercy. Not everyone welcomes the idea of world dictators and
mass murderers repenting and being accepted in heaven, but who are we to say who
should and who shouldn't be saved by the Author of Life? After all, the apostle Paul led
a less than exemplary life before he met Jesus, and look at the new tricks that old
dog learnt.

It's never too late to repent and turn to you, Father, is it?
I am so grateful for the fresh start and new life you offer.

Ask the boss!

Trust in the LORD with all your heart and lean not on your own understanding;
in all your ways acknowledge him, and he will make your paths straight.
Proverbs 3:5-6 (NIV)

●

When I was growing up, we had a ginger tomcat called Paddy.

Like a lot of cats, Paddy would sometimes take it upon himself to present us with a still-living mouse, as a token of his affection. Needless to say, we were not impressed.

He'd spend hours mousing. He was extremely patient and persistent as he focused on his intended prey. Mousing may have pleased Paddy, but if he'd thought it through, he'd have caught a bar of milk chocolate for me, instead. If only he'd asked first; he'd have saved himself all that effort!

Don't you sometimes wish that you'd asked God what he wanted before setting out on some venture? I do. Too many times I've devoted myself to a project that I believe would please God and make life better. Usually, it's something I have a sudden whim about and I concentrate all my creative thoughts on planning how wonderful it's going to be. All too often, I run out of enthusiasm before it gets off the ground, or if I do see it through, someone will gently point out that I've wasted my time trying to re-invent the wheel. It would have been far better to consult God first, of course, but you know how it is when you hit upon an idea...

How often do we do that, though? How often do we tell God what *we're* prepared to do for *him*, rather than ask him what *he* wants from *us*? It's all back-to-front and inside-out and then we wonder why it doesn't turn out right and why God hasn't helped us.

We need to pray, both alone and with others – especially with others – to seek God's will. And then we need to wait and listen to his response so we can act upon what he tells us.

Photo: Marlene Barnes

Oh dear; we're very fond of telling you what we want to do for you and then expecting you to help us achieve it, aren't we Father? Keep reminding me how it works; that we seek your will and serve you, not the other way around. I should know better by now. After all, you're the boss! Amen.

Ins-*purr*-ational QUOTES

The smallest feline is a masterpiece.

Leonardo da Vinci 1452–1519, Italian artist, sculptor and scientist

For a man to truly understand rejection, he must first be ignored by a cat.

Anon

No amount of time can erase the memory of a good cat, and no amount of masking tape can ever totally remove his fur from your couch.

Leo Dworken, author

Cats can work out mathematically the exact place to sit that will cause most inconvenience.

Pam Brown, author

There is no snooze button on a cat who wants breakfast.

Anon

With their qualities of cleanliness, discretion, affection, patience, dignity and courage, how many of us, I ask you, would be capable of becoming cats?

Fernand Mery 1897–1983, French author and vet

Perfect purr-suasion

...You have forsaken your first love.
Revelation 2:4 (NIV)

●

When it comes to the gentle art of purr-suasion, the cat's got it licked.

Independent and aloof most of the time, the common moggy is the master of manipulation, fooling us with purr-fect flattery when he or she wants help or attention.

You don't have to be a cat-owner to know what I mean – you will have seen it on the TV ads for cat food, or witnessed it first-hand at a friend's house.

Her majesty will stroll past, nose in the air, as if you're not worth spitting upon. Then, moments later, she will return and act as though you are the most important being in the world; the hub of her entire universe. She will unashamedly flirt with you – rubbing her head against you, wrapping her smooth, silky body around your legs, all the time purring in ecstasy.

And why this sudden display of love and veneration? Why, because she wants something of course. Food, milk, attention; it really doesn't matter, because as sure as eggs are eggs, once you've satisfied her every desire, she's off again, and suddenly you're not worthy of a sideways glance. In fact, you no longer exist as far as she is concerned.

That, believe it or not, is exactly how we treat God sometimes. We go about our day-to-day lives with scant regard for the Heavenly Father who provides for us. Until we need something, that is. And then we declare undying love and devotion, often promising the moon on a stick if God will meet our needs or entertain our whims and fancies.

And what happens once our prayer is answered favourably? We go joyfully on our way, relying on our own strength and ability and conveniently forgetting God's constant care and provision for us, until we need him again.

Fickle as felines, aren't we?

However do you put up with me, Lord? I'm so fickle, so shallow, so inconsistent. Forgive me, yet again, and help me to be more loyal and quicker to say thank you.

Photo: Marlene Barnes

Fear not

There is no fear in love. But perfect love drives out fear, because fear has
to do with punishment. The one who fears is not made perfect in love.
1 John 4:18 (NIV)

•

Honey's afraid of the Hoover.

At least I think it's false bravado that causes her to attack the vacuum cleaner each
time I use it. Either that or she senses that I hate hoovering and is trying to eradicate
a little misery from my life. Then again, I also hate cleaning the oven, but she's never
sunk her teeth into the cooker.

Photo: Kitsen

It's probably the noise she doesn't like. It doesn't appear to be any one vacuum cleaner in particular: we've had several over the years and she's shown equal animosity to each. If only she realised that it's a good thing. It's beneficial to the cleanliness of our home, but Honey doesn't see it that way. To her, it's a threat.

How can I show her that it's a friend, not a foe? Perhaps I should buy it a collar and take it on walks with us. Or maybe I could give it a bone and tickle its tummy. I've played the dirty-house-grumpy-owner, clean-house-happy-owner card, but that hasn't worked. An irrational fear can be a common problem with dogs, but it's hardly a matter of life and death.

People's fearful mistrust of anything Christian however, is a different matter. You know what I mean; people mocking Christians and Christ himself, because really, deep down, they're scared of his life-giving power. Admittedly, some of them think it's utter foolishness, but a lot of people scoff because they're afraid of being changed for the better. They're frightened of losing control; irrationally frightened of being brainwashed and becoming mindless automatons.

Our job is to show them that this couldn't be further from the truth. Far from becoming robots, Christians are set free to become the people God wants us to be. He loves us into being. He uses our individuality, our gifts and talents, and in him we are fulfilled individuals with a strong sense of what is right and good and true. As his followers, let's endeavour to share that sense of peace and fulfilment with the rest of the world and to show people that God is their friend, not their foe.

Jesus, friend of sinners, may our light shine brightly in the world so that others can see that in your perfect love there is freedom, not fear.

Canine QUIPS

Every boy should have two things: a dog, and a mother willing to let him have one.

Anon

There is no psychiatrist in the world like a puppy licking your face.

Ben Williams

Did you ever walk into a room and forget why you walked in?
I think that is how dogs spend their lives.

Sue Murphy

Dogs are not our whole life, but they make our lives whole.

Roger Caras 1928–2001, American activist

Old age means realizing you will never own all the dogs you wanted to.

Joe Gores 1931–2011, American mystery writer

Dogs laugh, but they laugh with their tails.

Max Eastman 1883–1969, American writer

A dog teaches a boy fidelity, perseverance,
and to turn around three times before lying down.

Robert Benchley 1889–1945, American humourist

Photo: Suzie Bacon

Sibling rivalry

*...whoever wants to become great among you must be your servant,
and whoever wants to be first must be your slave...*
Matthew 20:26-27 (NIV)

Walking our terrible twosome isn't always as relaxing as it should be. Our daily constitutional brings out Blossom's highly developed competitive side and believe me, it's extremely wearing.

I think it's all to do with security, or rather, the lack of it. Whereas Honey is laid-back and has no ambition to be top dog, Blossom is desperate to be number one. At home, she has to make sure she barks first, gobbles down her food first, is made a fuss of first. Out and about, she strives to be first through gateways, first up hills and is determined to 'water' more blades of grass than all the other dogs in the village. She pulls on her lead continually as she struggles to be a nose ahead of Honey.

If only she wouldn't try so hard! We'd all enjoy our 'walkies' far more – herself included – if she wasn't so focused on being first all the time.

Jesus had the same problem with James and John. Was it insecurity driving them to seek positions as Head Boys in heaven? Jesus put them in their place, explaining that it is humility and servitude that reaps rewards in heaven, as opposed to status and self-seeking behaviour, which leads nowhere in his kingdom.

Unhealthy competitiveness can rear its head at any time and in any place, even in the church. Who creates the best flower arrangement? Who has got the clearest reading voice? Whose intercessions are the most eloquent? And so on and so forth. Ridiculous, isn't it?

God isn't in the business of handing out rosettes for personal achievements. He's more interested in seeing us get stuck into the work he's ordained for us – serving one another and pointing others towards the ever-open door to his kingdom.

Remember; the bigger your head, the more difficult it is to fit through the doorway!

Photo: Jo Harris

Well, Lord, you certainly know how to keep our feet on the ground! Please help us to stay focused on the task in hand – serving you and one another, so that we forget ourselves and in so doing, advance your kingdom here on earth.

Mouse in the house of God

So be strong and courageous! Do not be afraid and do not panic before them.
For the LORD your God will personally go ahead of you. He will neither
fail you nor abandon you.
Deuteronomy 31:6 (NLT)

●

I saw him during the first hymn.

Was it a trick of the light or had a mouse just scampered out from behind the organ? Two things you need to know. Firstly, I'm a Reader in the Anglican ministry and I was leading the service and secondly, I'm jump-on-a-chair afraid of rodents.

Photo: Tamara Bauer

Another glance at the ground confirmed my fears were spot on. A small emboldened field mouse was taking a leisurely stroll across the red carpet.

Tempting though it was to drop everything and run, I had a job to do. I had no option but to stay put, I continued to warble 'Fight the Good Fight' though flight the good flight would have been more acceptable under the circumstances! Two more verses to go and Mouse was getting ever closer.

I stamped my feet, hoping to scare him off, but Mouse wasn't perturbed. Time to start praying. Lord, if you want me to stay here and continue with this service, please make him go away.

I could see his eyes – two shiny black beads – and his delicate little paws. His fur shone in the sunlight that streamed in through the window. Something strange was happening. Far from being frightened, I found myself admitting that there was something undeniably cute about this little animal.

I could see why most people aren't scared of them. He was an engaging creature with the 'Ahhh' rather than the 'Aaaaaaaagh!' factor.

I didn't want him coming any closer, but his presence was bearable.

In that moment, God's promise to walk before us, always on hand and never far away, rang as true as it had when he'd spoken to the Israelites thousands of years ago. He continues to speak to those who listen, giving hope and encouragement for all of life's situations and providing us with the strength to cope with circumstances that we never thought we could endure.

Lord, you are so wise! Instead of removing life's problems,
you give us the ability to face up to and overcome them,
and what's more, you walk beside us all the way! Thank you.

Paws for  **THOUGHT**

An animal's eyes have the power to speak a great language.

Martin Buber 1878–1965, German philosopher and interpreter

•

Animals are such agreeable friends – they ask no questions, they pass no criticisms.

George Eliot 1819–1880, English Victorian novelist

•

If having a soul means being able to feel love and loyalty and gratitude,
then animals are better off than a lot of humans.

James Herriot 1916–1995, Scottish vet and author

•

Animals are reliable, many full of love, true in their affections, predictable in their
actions, grateful and loyal. Difficult standards for people to live up to.

Alfred A. Montapert 1906–1997, American motivational author

•

He prayeth best, who loveth best all things both great and small;
For the dear God who loveth us, he made and loveth all.

Samuel Taylor Coleridge 1772–1834, English poet

All miracles, great and small

"Unless you people see miraculous signs and wonders,"
Jesus told him, "you will never believe."
John 4:48 (NIV)

●

Last year, I spent a week in the Lake District with my husband. Our hotel sat in extensive grounds that included dense woodland. Every morning, a group of us would venture into the woods to witness a colony of red squirrels feeding on the peanuts provided by the hotel staff.

Although I love wildlife, I was not as excited as I should be, watching these delightful creatures dine. The reason for my lack of enthusiasm is, I must confess, both mulish and ungracious; namely that I did not stumble upon them myself. Had I spotted a red squirrel unexpectedly, I would have felt privileged; the moment would have been something special. As it was, someone had done all the groundwork for me and I felt short-changed.

You're probably thinking that I'm an ungrateful, idiotic so-and-so. Quite right, I am. My attitude got me thinking, however. Are we sometimes guilty of looking for the more spectacular signs of God's grace and majesty and in so doing, failing to recognise – or acknowledge – his splendour in the 'familiar miracles' that are part of daily life?

Take healing as an example. We have become so used to the wonderful work carried out by the medical profession that we hardly recognise the miracle involved. Taking an aspirin to relieve the symptoms of a headache, or antibiotics to cure a chest infection, may not seem spectacular when compared with miracles of the pick-up-your-bed-and-walk variety, but miracles they are, nonetheless. And in nature, every caterpillar that turns into a butterfly and every bulb that blossoms into a spring flower is, in its own way, a special miracle from God.

Our God is a generous God, and when you start to look, examples of his love and power are evident for all to see. There will still be those who refuse to believe unless a miraculous sign drops from the sky into their laps, but while they're waiting, perhaps we can help them to look at the world with new eyes.

And when someone believes, that, in itself, is a miracle of God's grace.

Photo: Mike Williams

Oh Lord, sometimes we can't see the wood for the trees!
Open our eyes to your many blessings. And help us to show others
that your hand is at work in everything that is good and true.

Called by name

The gatekeeper opens the gate for him; the sheep hear his voice
as he calls his own sheep by name, and he leads them out.
John 10:3 (GNB)

●

It's always a privilege to name an animal, though the novelty probably wore off for Noah when faced with so many different species, (Genesis 2:19). I guess he'd reached the end of the alphabet when he named the zebra.

Whenever *Blue Peter*, the children's television programme, has a new pet, the young viewers are invited to send in their suggestions for a new name and they take part in their tens of thousands. There was once a front-page scandal when it was revealed that a kitten, named Socks by the team, should have been called Cookie, the name that was chosen by the majority of children. Choosing names is a serious business.

We gave our hamster an alliterative name: Hattie the Hamster. We could have chosen a name to describe her appearance – Toffee, or a name to describe her behaviour – Speedy, or even named her after her favourite food – Cornflake. The possibilities were endless, but we chose Hattie because it just seemed to suit her and if we went to her cage and called her name she'd pop her nose out to see if we had brought her anything interesting.

God knows the names of each of his children, just imagine that. You can probably name our royal family by sight, but do they know your name? Not a hope. Yet God, the Creator of the universe, calls you by name.

God knew you before you were born, he knows everything about you, "even the very hairs of your head are all numbered." (Matthew 10:30). And God not only knows your name, but he has inscribed it on his hand. "See, I have written your name on the palms of my hands." (Isaiah 49:16).

When we had a second hamster named Cocoa, I persistently called her Hattie – I guess I'm a creature of habit with a very poor memory! Yet God, the all-powerful

God of the whole massive universe, knows my name and your name – and he knows us and loves us individually and completely and never ever forgets us. Isn't that an overwhelming thought?

Photo: Marlene Barnes

Lord, the world is full of so many people and yet you know each of your children by name and invite us to call you Father. Thank you that you know every detail about us, good and bad, and yet you still go on loving us.

Ins-*purr*-ational
QUOTES

I have studied many philosophers and many cats.
The wisdom of cats is infinitely superior.

Hippolyte Taine 1828–1893, French critic and historian

•

Women and cats will do as they please, and men
and dogs should relax and get used to the idea.

Anon

•

If a dog jumps in your lap, it is because he is fond of you;
but if a cat does the same thing, it is because your lap is warmer.

Alfred North Whitehead 1861–1947, English mathematician and philosopher

•

Cats leave pawprints on our hearts.

Anon

•

Cats' names are more for human benefit. They give one a certain
degree more confidence that the animal belongs to you.

Alan Ayckbourn 1939–present day, English playwright

INSTRU
TIPS VOO
CONSEILS

1. Open all flaps of the
De kleppen van de d
Ouvrir les rabats

2. Turn the box upside d
De doos verschuiven o
Retourner le carton

3. Remove the box.
De doos optillen.
Soulever le carton.

Photo: Marlene Barnes

Free to choose

Now the Lord is the Spirit, and where the Spirit of the Lord is, there is freedom.
2 Corinthians 3:17 (NIV)

●

Our family kitten ran away before I was born – by this you'll deduce that I was in no way to blame!

My sister was nearly three when the kitten arrived in our home and she loved him with all her being. However, the little kitten didn't really enjoy this relentless adoration and took to rushing out of the door each time my sister walked in! He really didn't like being hugged quite so frequently or tightly and soon left home in search of a quieter life.

My sister was desperate to love and be loved by this little kitten, but she made the mistake of holding him too tightly and denying him any freedom.

God loves us totally and completely, but he doesn't hang on to us or restrict us in any way. He allows us to choose whether to love him or not. He gives us the freedom to live our lives just as we choose, with him or without him. He wants us to turn to him willingly, of our own accord, and then he'll know that our love is genuine, unshackled and freely given.

In Bizet's opera, Carmen sings that *Love is like a wild bird that no one can tame*, but if a bird is given the freedom to fly away and yet still returns to you then you'll know it truly loves you. Perhaps God feels like that about his children. He could force us to love him, but he'd far rather set us free and let us make our own choices. Then, when we return to him, it's because we have made our own decision to love and follow him and not because we are forced to do so.

Lord, it's good to know that you love us utterly and completely and yet you still give us the freedom to make our own decisions. Help us to make wise choices.

Happy hounds

Obey me, and I will be your God and you will be my people.
Walk in obedience to all I command you, that it may go well with you.
Jeremiah 7:23 (NIV)

●

Our dogs are not the best-trained mutts in the world. They've learnt the basics: Sit, Stay – if I catch them in the right mood – Walkies and Wee-wees (yes, they will empty their bladders before bed or before we go out), but it's just as well I don't have an overriding ambition to appear on *Britain's Got Talent* with dancing dogs.

I admire a well-trained dog; those who walk to heel regardless of what's going on around them. If I were to let my hounds off the lead in a field they'd go chasing after rabbits or deer, or anything else that moves – a leaf, a paper bag or even a shadow. Yet some dogs are so obedient they wouldn't bat an eyelid if a mouse kicked sand in their face.

A well-trained dog is a happy dog. It knows its place in the pecking order; it knows what's expected of it. It is secure and fulfilled.

Dogs are pack animals. They flourish under a leader who can bring out the best in them. They delight in pleasing their master. In just the same way we humans need a leader to bring us to a place of security, fulfilment and peace. That leader is God.

Look at our world and you'll see people fending for themselves, or in small groups, fighting and squabbling, lost and frightened as they scavenge for spiritual food in all the wrong places. Are they happy, living out this dog-eat-dog existence?

True happiness comes from the realisation that the God who loves us into being is the one we should follow with loyal and joyful obedience. He alone can teach us how to live disciplined, fulfilling lives and to behave as a well co-ordinated pack of disciples, respecting one another, working together and aiming to please our true Lord and Master.

Happy are those, Lord, who put their trust in you! Help us to show the lost and lonely, the frightened and insecure, that under your guidance and leadership we can fulfil our potential and find perfect peace. May your pack increase in number.

Photo: Marlene Barnes

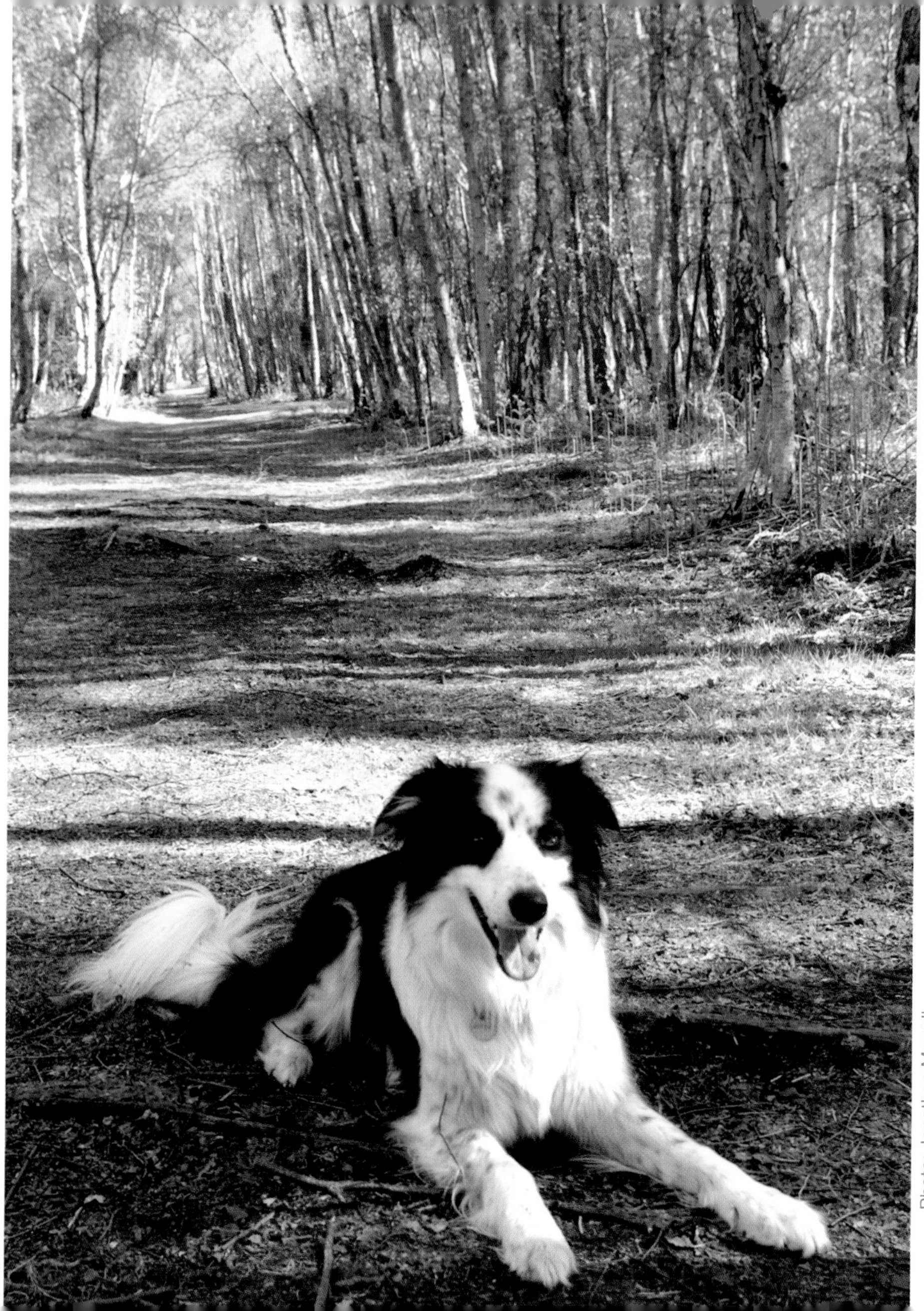

Photo: Jonathan Merrell

Canine QUIPS

A dog has lots of friends because he wags his tail and not his tongue.

Anon

●

To err is human, to forgive, canine.

Anon

●

No one appreciates the very special genius of your conversation as a dog does.

Christopher Morley 1890–1957, American author

●

You think dogs will not be in heaven?
I tell you, they will be there long before any of us.

Robert Louis Stevenson 1850–1894, Scottish author

●

A door is what a dog is perpetually on the wrong side of.

Ogden Nash 1902–1971, American poet

●

To sit with a dog on a hillside on a glorious afternoon is to be back in Eden,
where doing nothing was not boring – it was peace.

Milan Kundera 1929–present day, Czech author

Out of sight, out of mind?

O Lord, you have searched me and you know me. You know when I sit and when I rise; you perceive my thoughts from afar. You discern my going out and my lying down; you are familiar with all my ways.

Psalm 139:1-3 (NIV)

•

Our dogs – bless their little furry paws – must think I'm thick.

We have a 'humans only on furniture' policy in our household and, as long as we're around, the dogs abide by it. However, nip outside or upstairs and the terrible twosome grab their chance to jump up on the sofa or curl up in the rocking chair. Of course, they're quick to vacate their cosy seat before we return to the room.

They think we're far too dense to realise that the hair on the cushion is theirs or that the chair, still creaking and rocking, has anything to do with them.

At least they have the grace to look guilty.

It's the same with food. A morsel left on the kitchen worktop proves much too tempting when the master or mistress' back is turned. It's the slinking-quietly-out-of-the-kitchen that gives the game away.

I'll always remember the awed silence when my Sunday School teacher told us that God sees everything we do. "There's no point hiding under the bed covers if you've done something wrong," she informed us, "because God can still see you." Worrying stuff when you're ten years old and have broken your dad's hacksaw blade – especially when you shouldn't have been anywhere near it in the first place.

It's part of the eternal mystery and majesty of God that he is able to look upon everyone, every minute of every day. For those who've rejected his love, that's a cause for concern. For those who love God, however, it's a source of great comfort. How amazing it is, to know that God is keeping an ever-watchful eye on us wherever we are.

The King of all Creation is looking out for us. We have nothing to fear.

Photo: Tomasz Markowski

There really is nowhere to hide from your love, is there, Father? You know whatever we have said, done or thought and you still continue to love us. Thank you.

Heart-warming medicine

...God has poured out his love into our hearts by the Holy Spirit, whom he has given us.
Romans 5:5 (NIV)

It's official, cats are good for your health!

Researchers in America have discovered that owning a cat can reduce the risk of heart attacks and strokes by more than a third. Scientists said that having a cat helped to relieve stress and anxiety, which is known to help protect against heart disease by lowering blood pressure and reducing the heart rate.

It makes sense doesn't it? Gently stroking a sleepy cat is wonderful calming therapy – an antidote to a hectic lifestyle.

I had an aunt who would always have a few moments of calm first thing in the morning, a cup of tea by her side, gently stroking her cat on her lap while she talked to God.

It's great to start the day with God, to hand over all the joys, worries and forthcoming events into the care of our loving Father. He wants to fill our hearts with love and peace and the certain knowledge that he will be walking with us throughout the day. So when life is hectic and full of hassles, set aside a few minutes to hand everything over to God. You might just find that you cope better with the day ahead. It might even lower your blood pressure too!

And if you're a night owl, you might find that a quiet moment with God is heart-soothing therapy at the end of a tough day – and folk who have a calm cat with whom to share the experience are surely twice blessed!

Lord, sometimes life is manic and my heart and mind feel over-burdened. When this happens help me to stop, take stock and give my day to you. You always bring peace to my heart and help me to uncover the right priorities.

There are few things in life more heart-warming than to be welcomed by a cat.
Tony Hohoff, *author of* Cats and Other People

A meow massages the heart.
Stuart McMillan

Paws for  THOUGHT

The best thing about animals is that they don't talk much.

Thornton Wilder 1897–1975, American playwright

•

Until one has loved an animal, a part of one's soul remains unawakened.

Anatole France 1844–1924, French writer

•

The greatness of a nation and its moral progress can
be judged by the way its animals are treated.

Mahatma Gandhi 1869–1948, Indian political, spiritual leader and humanitarian

•

I care not for a man's religion whose dog and cat are not the better for it.

Abraham Lincoln 1809–1865, 16th President of the United States of America

•

I like pigs. Dogs look up to us. Cats look down on us. Pigs treat us as equals.

Winston Churchill 1874–1965, British Prime Minister

•

You are worthy, our Lord and God,
to receive glory and honour and power,
for you created all things,
and by your will they were created and have their being.

Revelation 4:11 (NIV)

Photo: David Davenport

Un-common sense

The LORD does not look at the things man looks at. Man looks at the
outward appearance, but the LORD looks at the heart.
1 Samuel 16:7 (NIV)

●

By now, you will have gathered that I am a dog-lover.

Imagine my surprise then, upon going to dinner at a colleague's house and finding that their new dog disliked me intensely. My hosts apologised about their pet's behaviour. Normally a friendly beast, Compo barked and growled at me and was promptly banished to another room so I could enjoy my meal without fear of losing a limb.

Dogs don't normally judge by appearance. Their sight is not as well-developed as ours. Their hearing is good and their sense of smell is sublime. But when it comes to people, dogs decide their likes and dislikes with some inner, highly individual sixth sense.

Our own dogs are rescue dogs. Choosing a dog from a rescue centre is a two-way process; the dog chooses you just as much as you choose the dog. As potential owners, we go on looks initially. If a dog looks appealing and has a waggy tail, we are drawn to it. Only then do we consider its disposition.

From the dog's perspective, looks are irrelevant. Short, tall, thin, fat, old, young; it makes no difference. All they care about is whether or not we are likely to be kind to them.

If only we humans were less obsessed by outward appearances! I know I'm guilty of judging folk on a first glance. That may well change as I get to know them, but put me in a room full of strangers and, like most people, I will gravitate towards the individual who looks most like 'my kind of person'.

Remember when Jesus went to dine at the tax collector's house? Matthew and his friends weren't the sort of people the Pharisees would choose to be seen with, but Jesus made it his business to seek out individuals who didn't rate highly in the popularity stakes. And James warned against showing favouritism to the richest-

looking people (James 2:3-4). We must learn to choose not with our eyes and our ears, but with the heart of love that God gave us.

And as for Compo, well it turned out that his previous owner had mistreated him. Her voice was, apparently, similar to mine and, who knows, perhaps we even wore the same perfume...?

Yes, Lord, I'm guilty. Guilty of choosing my friends by worldly standards.
Guilty of wanting to surround myself with 'my kind of people'.
That's not how you ordained it, is it? Sorry. Help me to be open
to the people you want me to meet and befriend.

A glorious inheritance

All praise to God, the Father of our Lord Jesus Christ. It is by his great mercy that we have been born again, because God raised Jesus Christ from the dead. Now we live with great expectation, and we have a priceless inheritance…

1 Peter 1:3-5 (NLT)

The much-loved and slightly eccentric English actress Beryl Reid was famous for her love of cats. When she died, her five feline friends: Hamish, Boon, Eileen, Coco and Tuffnel, inherited her home worth £1million. A friend was commissioned to look after them so they could continue to live in their own house!

Those fat-cats enjoyed life in the lap of luxury for the rest of their nine lives. So how does that make you feel, just a little bit green-eyed? It would be awesome to receive an unexpected inheritance wouldn't it? A sudden windfall, or a special mention in a will.

As believers, we too have a glorious inheritance, but there's nothing unexpected about it. It is one that we have been promised. We are told to expect it and we can enjoy anticipating it and, when it comes, our inheritance will last for ever. When people die, they frequently leave an inheritance for their living relatives left behind, but for Christians, it is only after their own death that they receive their glorious inheritance.

We are promised that those who believe in Jesus will receive the joy of eternal life in heaven with him. So, we can live in hope, knowing that the next life is even better than this one. And if heaven is half as amazing as we're told, I guess Christians can be thankful that they don't have nine lives. Why keep heaven waiting?

So pass on the good news and share the inheritance, so that those you love don't miss out.

Lord Jesus, thank you that you treat us like close family and promise us a special inheritance. We don't deserve it. Keep reminding us to tell others that they can inherit your kingdom too.

Father of the world,
all things were created by you.
Thank you for the companionship of animals,
each one was perfectly designed and created by you.
Thank you for the special joy they bring into our lives.
Help us to show them compassion and kindness.

Father, hear and bless
Thy beasts and singing birds;
And guard with tenderness
Small things that have no words.

Traditional

A dog's letter to his master

Love the LORD your God with all your heart and with
all your soul and with all your strength.
Deuteronomy 6:5 (NIV)

•

Dear Master

I'm writing to you to say 'sorry' for eating those pretzels. I know it was wrong of me, but you left them on the coffee table when you went out and I just couldn't help myself. The spirit is willing but the body is weak, as you say. Anyway, I'm really sorry.

I know that there are other things that annoy you. I know you get irritated when I follow you everywhere, but it's only because I love you so much and want to spend as much time as possible with you. And you don't like it when I lick you, do you? That too, is because I love you. I can't hug you or stroke you like you do to me; licking is all I can do. And when you come home from work, I can't help barking and squeaking and bouncing up and down; I'm so pleased to see you that I want to tell the whole world how wonderful you are.

I really enjoy our walks. I know I pull on my lead, but I want you to visit all my favourite places and to smell all my favourite smells. Having you with me when I discover something new is special.

You get annoyed if I bark in the night, don't you? I'm sorry. It's just that sometimes I get anxious when I hear a noise outside and I need to wake you up so you can tell me everything's all right.

And when it comes to food, you must think I'm a right greedy guts. You give me more than enough, and I appreciate it, I really do. But when you drop some of your human food, I see it as a special treat. I am glad to eat the crumbs from under your table.

I'd do anything within my power to make you happy because I love and respect you with all my life. I will always do my best to please you.

Your affectionate hound,

Buster

Photo: Starblue

Dear Lord, there's a lot we can learn from our pets, isn't there? Help us to be more like our dogs – devoted, loyal and always eager to follow and please you.

Don't accept your dog's admiration as conclusive
evidence that you are wonderful.
Ann Landers, *American fictional advice columnist*

●

A dog is the only thing on earth that will love you more than you love yourself.
Josh Billings *1818–1885, pen name of the American humourist and writer Henry Wheeler Shaw*

A cat's letter to her mistress

And because of God's gracious gift to me I say to every one of you: do not think of yourself more highly than you should. Instead, be modest in your thinking, and judge yourself according to the amount of faith that God has given you.

Romans 12:3 (GNB)

•

Dear Serv...... 'Mistress'

First and foremost, I am not ordinarily one for revealing my emotions, so consider yourself honoured that I see fit to educate you in this manner.

Photo: Annette Love

A few points for your consideration:

1. When I am sleeping, kindly refrain from waking me. I have no wish to be disturbed according to your whims.

2. Should it be raining, sleeting or snowing, make no attempt to 'entice' me outside.
I refuse to get my paws cold and/ or wet for your convenience. On the occasion that it may be necessary for me to empty bladder and/or bowels, I will decide the where and when.

3. If I desire to catch rodents and birds, I will. Whether or not you approve is of no interest to me. You have your fun and I shall have mine.

4. Hmm. The not-so-small matter of sustenance. Refrain, if you will, from serving up inferior quality meat and

do ensure that food that has been in the refrigerator has attained room temperature before it reaches my plate.

5. Do not be so vain as to expect a rousing welcome each time you return to the household. I frequently have more important matters to consider than pandering to your delicate ego.

I daresay you think I fail to appreciate your meagre efforts to keep me in the style to which I am accustomed. Much as it pains me, I confess that you do, in fact, serve a purpose. However, if I could operate the can-opener myself, I would have no further need of you.

For now,

Your (Superior) Feline Acquaintance, *Lady Esmeralda Windsor*.

PS Do make an effort to use my proper name; 'Sweetie-pie' does grate somewhat.

Dear Father, forgive me for the times I treat you like that – ungracious, ungrateful, proud and arrogant. I need and depend upon you for everything. Thank you for all that you do for me. I do love you – I just don't tell you often enough.

You can keep a dog; but it is the cat who keeps people,
because cats find humans useful domestic animals.
George Mikes 1912–1987, Hungarian-born British author

●

There are many intelligent species in the universe. They are all owned by cats.
Anon

●

Dogs have owners, cats have staff.
Anon

In the  NEWS

A woman was on the phone to a pet supply company and she was right in the middle of ordering a cat flap to be installed in her kitchen door, when she put the phone down without any warning. Five minutes later she rang the company again, "I'm so sorry that I put the phone down on you," she explained, "only the cat walked in and the cat flap is a surprise birthday present, so I didn't want her to overhear our conversation."

•

A dog was hailed as a hero after it risked its life to save a litter of newborn kittens from a house fire. Leo, the terrier cross, had to be revived with oxygen and heart massage after his ordeal. Fire broke out overnight at the house in Melbourne, Australia, where brave Leo was guarding the kittens. Firefighters said "Leo wouldn't leave the kittens and it nearly cost him his life."

•

Boris the cat attempted to order 450 cans of his favourite food on an internet shopping site while his owner wasn't looking. His owner had already ordered six cans – apparently Boris didn't think that was enough.

•

A woman whose cat had gone missing a few hours earlier was astonished find out that it had made an impromptu appearance on the TV programme, *Question Time*. The programme was being recorded at a community college in Newquay, close to where Jackie, the owner, lives. She was wondering where Tango had got to when he walked into shot behind the host and his panel of MPs. "My friend phoned me to say, 'Have you seen your cat on the telly?' And there he was," said Jackie.

•

At Kansas zoo, three white tiger cubs were abandoned by their real mother just a day after birth, but Isabella, a golden retriever, is doing a terrific job as surrogate mum and the cubs are growing quickly. Isabella doesn't seem to mind a bit, she even cleans up her little cubs and licks them into shape.

Thank you, Lord, for the gift of pets to share our lives.
Thank you for the love and laughter they bring into our homes.
Thank you for their courage and compassion in special situations.
Thank you for their warm hearts and listening ears.
Amen

Photo: Helen Sharpe

For all things were created by him, and all things exist through him and for him.
To God be the glory for ever! Amen.
Romans 11:36 (GNB)

Where the grass is greener

I have learned the secret of being content in any and every situation,
whether well fed or hungry, whether living in plenty or in want.
I can do everything through him who gives me strength.
Philippians 4:12-13 (NIV)

•

Our neighbours have a manic dog!

Cassie is so active that they reckon she has the doggy equivalent of ADHD. Cassie loves to run and jump and chase and chew. And to prove it, she's chewed right through our fence in numerous places. Our dog-tired neighbours have already reinforced the bottom of the fence right around the garden, so Cassie now chews higher up. As soon as she has made a big enough hole, she pops through and joyfully bounces into our garden to check us out.

I kid myself that Cassie likes us and wants to come and say hello, but she's actually chewed through the fences on all three sides of her garden and checked out all the neighbouring gardens! For Cassie, the grass on the other side of the fence is definitely greener and she is determined not to miss out. She always wants to scale the next height, turn the next corner, investigate the next dustbin! She's always on the go and never content to just rest and enjoy the moment.

Some folk are a bit like that too, they are never quite satisfied. They always have one eye on the next promotion, a bigger house, a faster computer, a newer sofa. The grass on the neighbour's side of the fence is definitely greener and they are keen not just to keep up with the Joneses but hopefully to overtake them too.

It's very easy to be so concerned about reaching the next level, that you miss out on the pleasure and enjoyment of the present moment. It's rather like climbing a steep hill with your eyes permanently on the summit, sometimes it's good to stop en route to enjoy the climb and appreciate the view. So don't rush to scale the next height, but stop regularly to count your blessings. Look for everything that's good in your life now and savour the moment. It won't last forever.

PS: Scientists have pointed out that grass will always look greener when viewed from a distance!

Lord, we humans are sometimes very discontented, help us to find contentment in all the good things that bless our lives.

Don't bite off more than you can chew!

…Martha was distracted by the big dinner she was preparing. She came to Jesus and said, "Lord, doesn't it seem unfair to you that my sister just sits here while I do all the work? Tell her to come and help me."

But the Lord said to her, "My dear Martha, you are worried and upset over all these details! There is only one thing worth being concerned about. Mary has discovered it, and it will not be taken away from her."

Luke 10:40-42 (NLT)

●

Some years ago we had a hamster; she was small and fluffy with tan-and-white fur and we named her Hattie. One day, when we were quite new hamster parents, she filled her pouches with a huge chunk of apple that distorted her whole face from left to right in a most alarming way.

Photo: Marlene Barnes

Hattie tried to escape to her house but her cheeks were too big to fit through the door. She tried to hide in her cardboard tube but no, her cheeks were too wide. Eventually she disappeared under her ladder, and with a good deal of wriggling and tugging, she managed to extricate the fruit. Crisis over. However, from that day on, we cut up her food into smaller pieces, since she clearly had a habit of biting off far more than she could chew.

Some humans are just the same. They say "Yes" to so many things, agree to help with so much, that their whole life becomes over burdened and they know that they have bitten off more than they can chew. When someone rings up asking for help, it's hard to say "No". When the church is asking for volunteers, it's hard to ignore the plea.

Photo: Derek Cooper

Remember Martha in the Bible story; she was so busy rushing about preparing for the arrival of Jesus and his disciples that she became hassled and harassed and unable to take time to sit with Jesus and listen to him once he had arrived. Her 'To Do' list had got quite out of hand and she needed to stop and prioritize.

It's impossible to do everything, so take a deep breath before saying "Yes" and sometimes be ready to say "No, not this time". And why not involve God in the decision-making? Pray about which things are important and what might be better left to someone else. After all, God doesn't want a church full of burnt-out Christians; he cares about his children and every aspect of their lives.

Lord it's so easy to say "Yes" to everyone and everything and to bite off more than we can comfortably chew. Help us to stop, take stock and work out our priorities so that we leave room in our lives for you.

*Father God, Creator of all animals, big and small,
thank you for giving us such a rich variety of pets
to bless our lives with their loyalty and love
and to enrich our lives with their company and friendship.*